BEGONE, SATAN!

Our Sunday Visitor, Inc.
Huntington, Ind. 46750

Nihil Obstat:
Rev. Lawrence Gollner
Censor Librorum

Imprimatur:
✠ Leo A. Pursley, D.D.
Bishop of Fort Wayne-South Bend

February 15, 1974

ISBN: 0-87973-760-3
Library of Congress Catalog Card Number: 74-76903

Cover Design by James E. McIlrath and John Zierten

Published, printed and bound in the U.S.A. by
Our Sunday Visitor, Inc.
Noll Plaza,
Huntington, Indiana 46750
760

Begone, Satan!

CONTENTS

Pertinent Definitions

exorcism (Gr. *exorkizein,* bind with an oath) 1. The expelling of evil spirits in cases of possession and obsession according to the rite prescribed in the Roman Ritual, and presently performed by a priest with the permission of his bishop. 2. Lesser exorcisms are used in the ceremony of Baptism and in blessing water and salt. This exorcism does not imply possession.

exorcist The second of the minor orders which in the past gave the recipient power to expel the devil in the ceremony of exorcism and to take charge of the water needed for divine service. Exorcisms today are reserved to priests. In the Eastern Orthodox Church, exorcists are not ordained.

possession A word used in a very limited sense to indicate the possession or control of a person by a demon or demons. There are many instances in the Gospel narrative of demoniacal possession. The Church recognizes its existence in its ritual of exorcism. Only a priest can exorcise a possessed person and then only with the permission of his ordinary. Possession is not necessarily the result of sin or a pact with the devil for God permits it to occur in an innocent party. There are numerous cases of possession on record but the Church seldom makes any official judgment on whether they are real instances or not.

devil (L. *diabolus*) 1. A fallen angel. A purely spiritual being cut off from God because of the sin of rebellion. 2. An evil spirit, such as those driven out by Christ. 3. Lucifer, the chief of the rebellious angels who goes through the world like "a roaring lion seeking whom he may devour" (1 Pt. 5:8). He is a rational spirit, embittered over his loss of the Beatific Vision, who has turned to an unending hatred of God and things holy.

— **The Maryknoll Catholic Dictionary**

The Devil and Anna Ecklund
by John Patrick Gillese

1

EARLY in 1974, the news media uncovered
the case of an exorcism of diabolic obsession
that had taken place the previous fall in Daly
City, California. The press reported at length
and it was a subject of a number of television
talk shows which featured the exorcist, Father
Karl Patzelt, a Jesuit. All of this much to the
consternation of the Archbishop of San Francisco, who following Church practice, wanted
silence on the whole matter.

The case was brought to the attention of
the Jesuit by a group of Carmelite Sisters who
knew the family involved. The father was a
29-year-old transportation worker, his wife
was 26, and they had a two-year-old baby.
For two years the family had been under attack in ways that defied explanation and al-

though the family had moved twice, the evil spirits had followed them.

Not only was their family life destroyed but their health was being seriously undermined because the attacks went on day after day, for twenty-two hours a day. Only between 4 a.m. and 6 a.m. was the family able to get any sleep because for some strange reason, nothing happened in those hours.

When Father Patzelt entered the case, he described what he found: "There were broken windows, damaged walls, ceilings and doors dented and scraped, caused by flying objects such as shoes, knives, a poker and any other object the devil could grab. There were many articles burnt in the house. Rugs, wallpaper, curtains, chairs — even a dress worn by the wife which caught on fire while she walked down the hall."

Father Patzelt witnessed some of the phenomena himself. He saw the wife pushed to the ground with her arm extended in a rigid position.

"Where is my wedding ring?" she asked, when she got up. "It's gone. He took it."

The group then smelled something burning. They rushed into the kitchen. A paper bag, set aside for trash, was smoldering ashes. Then the baby started to cry upstairs. Mother, father and priest hurried up.

"When we entered the little boy's room," Father Patzelt said, "we found him in the corner of his crib obviously frightened. Somehow his little rocking chair had been lifted into his crib from where it had stood on the floor."

On the basis of his own observations and all that the parents told him, Father Patzelt submitted a detailed report to Archbishop Joseph T. McGucken of San Francisco, asking permission to perform an exorcism. The Archbishop consented and gave Father Patzelt Latin and English exorcism rituals, a relic of the true cross and another of St. John Vianney (the Curé of Ars), who himself had suffered from attacks by devils.

The exorcisms began on August 19 with the final exorcism on September 18. During the exorcisms, husband and wife were invisibly attacked, several times to the point of unconsciousness. As the exorcisms progressed, the night disturbances ended but attacks continued during the day. Since the final exorcism on September 18, the family has been completely at peace, looking back at the nightmare they went through, and wondering why it happened to them.

"The devil does not bother those who are already under his influence," Father Patzelt says. "He has no need to bother them. The devil came to this family to test their faith in God."

Perhaps a more oblique explanation lies in the fact that the husband had been brought up an Orthodox Jew and converted to Catholicism, the religion of his wife. McCandlish Phillips, prize-winning reporter of the New York *Times,* has made a detailed study called

The Bible, the Supernatural and the Jews (Bethany Fellowship, Inc.), in which he holds the thesis that the Jews have a very unique relationship with God. He points out that when a Jew becomes spiritually corrupt, he becomes excessively corrupt. It follows the old axiom of Thomas Aquinas that when the best is corrupted, it becomes the worst. The reverse can also be true. When a Jew embraces Christianity, he adopts a faith that has long stood in opposition to "the devil and all his pomps." Thus a Jewish convert might well earn the special hatred of Lucifer who is the natural enemy of Jesus Christ.

The sort of phenomena that happened in Daly City is anything but new. The Germans refer to the *poltergeist* — literally, "noisy ghost" — and certainly one such *poltergeist* made the front pages of almost all U.S. daily newspapers, got investigated by more scientific authorities than probably any other "ghost" in America, and even got a write-up in the pages of *The Reader's Digest.* The consensus of scientific opinion is that you cannot explain the unexplainable!

The question that troubles all but the most sophisticated (and perhaps secretly even them) is whether or not such a phenomena are the works of the devil.

"The devil's deepest wile is to persuade us he doesn't exist," said Baudelaire — and the truth of that statement is widespread today. To admit you believe in the devil is enough to create vast amusement in any modern audience. People are fascinated by the subject, as witness the success of *The Exorcist*. But they are sceptical about explanations.

Some sincere students of "psychic phenomena" state simply that you will only find a *poltergeist* wherever you find a boy or girl entering puberty — the implication being that such a youth somehow releases a form of psychosomatic energy that causes objects to fly around a room, the familiar loud noises, etc. These researchers — and there is overwhelming evidence to suggest they are close to the truth — maintain there is nothing supernatural whatsoever in such *poltergeist* activity.

On the other hand, there is an abundance of evidence — not to mention logic — to indicate that Lucifer does exist — and that he is as busy as ever, even in a modern world.

Logically speaking, if the devil did not exist, then Christianity exists on a very thin fabric. Who tempted Adam to fall? Who tempted Christ in the desert? Whose powers were overcome by the Crucifixion of Christ on Calvary?

Quite aside from the philosophical, there is abundant evidence, not only of Lucifer's existence, but even of his possession of men. Chinese and other missionaries have seen astonishing examples of diabolic possession; and the noted historian Léon Christiani, in *Présence de Satan dans le monde moderne,* has compiled documented evidence of Lucifer's "visible" activities from the days of the Curé d'Ars to people still living.

2

A TYPICAL case of diabolic activity was witnessed in 1906 by a Mariannhill priest, Father Erasmus Hoerner, stationed at St. Michael's Mission in South Africa. This well-documented incident revolved around a native girl, Germana Cele, and is fairly representative of all such stories of diabolic possession.

Father Hoerner received an urgent call to "do something" about this girl who periodically was seized by some sort of "fit." Her body would twist and contort. She would throw herself about her room, gnashing her teeth and raving. All who had any contact with her swore that, when these wild attacks seized her, sounds as of two different people arguing seemed to emanate through her foaming lips.

Nor were these the exaggerations of imaginative natives. A Sister Juliana, director of the settlement house, informed Father Hoerner that when she first found Germana in this condition, she had sprinkled the girl with holy water. Miss Cele went into a worse state than ever. "Sister!" she screamed. "You are burning me! Call Father Erasmus — he is the only one who can help me! It is Satan — he has power over me now!"

Recalling the case, Father Erasmus remembered a story of Germana "pledging" herself to the devil about a month before. He had not paid too much attention to the matter, specifically because the natives, most of them recent converts from fanciful pagan religions, were easily worked up emotionally. Likewise, it was possible that the girl was suffering a mental disorder. The last thing even a priest is apt to suppose is that any such person is actually in the power of the devil.

When he entered Germana Cele's house, however, it was evident that here was no ordinary emotional upset. Even in his presence, the girl continued to mutter and rave, till Father Hoerner spoke to her sharply.

"Germana, listen to me —"

"I am not Germana," a gutteral voice — from Germana, but not Germana's answered.

This was followed by a burst of shrieking laughter that ended only when the priest asked Germana:

"Who are you, then?"

"I am Satan," answered the voice. "Our king is Lucifer. His pride is great. We were driven from heaven to hell, though our sins were not as great as those of most men."

What makes the case of Germana Cele remarkable is that, in this African mission, the girl's inhuman ravings — and, later, her violent bodily contortions — were witnessed even publicly, at Mass. The tormented creature would beg to be freed; and a gutteral voice would growl from within her: "Germana keep silent! You are mine!"

On one occasion, even though guarded by several strong girls, she was completely uncontrollable. During Mass, she thrashed about, screamed, laughed diabolically and blasphemed at the Elevation of the Host. On this same occasion, during the Offertory, she manifested the final characteristic of those filled either with great holiness or gripped by diabolic possession:

Germana Cele soared bodily in mid-air, rising above the pews and floating towards the sanctuary.

It took stern commands from Father Erasmus to make her return to her place. Convinced beyond doubt that hers was a case of true diabolic possession, he applied to the Bishop for permission to conduct a solemn exorcism. On September 12, 1906, the ceremony began, with Father Erasmus and three other Mariannhill missionaries taking part. It was a simple case. After 24 hours, the struggle ended. Germana Cele was freed and, as far as the records show, was no longer bothered by Satan.

All cases of diabolic possession seem to follow the same pattern: growling "voices" — the ability to soar bodily about a room — wild, demonic rantings, ravings and struggles — and, usually, some unknown voice wherein the victim, or a delegate who speaks for the victim (a person's deceased father, for in-

14

stance) argues, bargains, or otherwise begs that Lucifer have power over that person.

Exceptions to this latter condition are found in the case of satanic manifestations at Ars, where the devil tormented Father (now Saint) Jean Baptiste Vianney; and at Lourdes and at other centers of miraculous apparitions, where it appears, the devil tries to sow sufficient confusion to destroy the validity of the apparitions. This, in fact, is an interesting and little-known aspect of Lucifer's activities.

At Lourdes, for example, Léon Christiani narrates how Bernadette herself declared that strange and unaccustomed noises disturbed one of the visions. There were many sounds seeming to echo and reply to each other. There were voices, questioning, contradicting, shouting, like many voices of a crowd in tumult. Amidst all these confusing voices, one more distinct than the rest could be heard uttering the furious and menacing cry: 'Flee! Flee!' "

Christiani chronicles the facts offering reasonable argument, quoting even the Mayor of Lourdes "on visionaries other than those seen by Bernadette Soubirous."

People of exceptionally good character and religious intuition "saw" the Blessed Virgin at many spots around the Grotto. But never, significantly, at the one spot where Bernadette had seen the Virgin. By late 1858, public confusion was at its height — which was precisely of course, what the devil wanted.

Christiani quotes the director who was in charge of the Lourdes as saying: "The devil prompted the appearance of a host of visionaries who indulged in the wildest extravagances. Did they really see anything? Yes, there is every reason to believe that many of them did see something, the Evil One, in various guises. Many of my pupils claimed to have seen visions. They often played truant. . . . These extravagances occurred not only in the Grotto and by a stream which runs close to the Basilica, but also in their own homes, where they improvised little chapels. . . .' "

3

IT IS the personal cases of diabolic possession, however, that have the most shattering
impact on people who will credit the com-
monsense and integrity of character of reli-
able chroniclers. In that respect, no case in the
United States can compare to the case "Anna
Ecklund." The name alone is fictitious —
used to protect an innocent victim of such
possession.

There are other cases. One took place in
Garrison, N.Y., under the exorcist Father
Theodosius Foley, O.F.M. Cap. Still another
— distorted and dramatized, as if that was
necessary — was the basis of *The Exorcist*.
But none had the documentation as that
which took place in rural Iowa.

To grasp the reality and the full story of
the devil and Anna Ecklund, you only have to
go back a few years — to September 1, 1928;
to the convent of the Franciscan Sisters in the
little town of Earling, Iowa — where the exorcism was about to begin.

The possessed woman was then 40 years
old. She lay fully clothed on the bare mattress
of a large old-fashioned iron bed, her dress
tightly secured as a precaution against im-

proper diabolical tricks — a measure warranted by some singular events of the preceding day.

First of all, on the train trip to Earling, the woman had fought like a woman possessed. The train crew — forewarned that she was subject to "fits" — got her to her destination with difficulty.

Due to meet the train, Father Joseph Steiger, parish priest of Earling, had a lot of trouble with his brand-new car. He was two hours late getting to the station, where he made profuse apologies to Mrs. Ecklund and the Rev. Theophilus Riesinger, O.F.M. Cap., the exorcist.

"No need to apologize, Father," said Father Riesinger. "No matter what happens, Mrs. Ecklund wants us to free her. You might as well start getting used to these things now."

They drove Anna Ecklund to the convent, where the Mother Superior received her and showed her to her room. The Sister-cook, ordered to prepare a tray of nourishing food, unthinkingly blessed it. The moment the serving Sister entered the room, Anna Ecklund sprang up on the bed, purring like a cat. Then, Anna Ecklund nearly strangled her. Not till they brought her unblessed food could the woman eat.

Now, tiny drops of perspiration beaded her forehead, though the Iowa morning was breeze-stirred and cool. The farmers — mostly of German extraction: generous, good-natured and unimaginative — were at work in the grain fields for it was harvest season.

Earling was quiet.

There was a light knock on Anna Ecklund's door. A young Sister, barely out of novitiate, entered the room, smiling nervously.

"Mrs. Ecklund, our morning Mass was specially offered for your intention. They're ready now. We'll all pray very hard for you."

The Mother Superior entered, followed by a veritable corps of Sisters. Two of them had been registered nurses before entering the religious life. All of them were strong, disciplined women. They fingered their long 15-decade Franciscan rosaries and took pre-arranged positions around Anna's bed.

With them was Father Joseph Steiger, who was to witness the incredible affair from beginning to end. It had been necessary to get his permission — as well as that of the Mother Superior — before the woman could even be brought into the parish, or the convent, for such a rite. The Bishop, as well as the exorcist, had felt obliged to warn Father Steiger solemnly over the possible consequences.

"The devil," said Father Riesinger "doesn't take this sort of interference lying down. The point is," went on the Capuchin, a lifelong friend of the pastor, "your parish seems the most suitable. Neither the woman, nor her family, could bear it in her home. It's quiet here, and far enough from where she lives so that she won't have to spend the rest of her life being pointed at as 'the woman who had a devil.' "

Father Steiger, perhaps understandably, hedged.

"I know we've gone over this before — but, Father Theo, this is 20th century Iowa!"

"And the woman's case of possession is genuine," Father Theophilus Riesinger said. "The Church moves too slowly for there to be any mistake."

"Maybe it's just a bad case of hallucination — or nerves . . ."

"Father, she's been suffering since she was a girl of 14." Exorcism was old stuff to Father Theophilus. "Add it up for yourself. A good and pious girl gets obsessed with the most unbelievable lusts — so distasteful to her she wants to hang herself. She wants to go to the Sacraments — and voices mock her — make her life hell. Year after year, every priest she goes to gives her the same advice: 'Go see a good doctor.' She's been to more than a dozen neurologists and psychiatrists — the best in Milwaukee and Chicago — and what do they say? There's nothing wrong with her — nothing at all! She gets married and her condition gets worse — far worse. The last time she forced herself to go to confession, for example, she got an urge to strangle the confessor. Then, of course, there's the business of tongues."

Anna Ecklund, the girl who never got past Grade Eight, who had never looked at anything more learned than a farm paper since, did not speak in tongues. She understood them. When her distraught husband begged the parish priest to drive out unclean spirits and bless their home, Anna kept screaming a literal translation of the Latin prayers. She presented a frightening picture of a woman who knew exactly what she was doing, yet was unable to help herself.

Faced with what the Church regards as final, unmistakable signs of diabolic possession, the Bishop re-examined the case — first presented to his office back in 1902, and added to by every pastor sent to Anna's parish over the intervening years. He decided he *had* to act.

Remembering the complaint of the Apostles that they were having trouble casting out devils — and Christ's rejoinder that it requires much penance and fasting to do so — his main task was to find a suitable exorcist. Finally he put the affair of Anna Ecklund completely in the care of a Capuchin already noted for his success in a dozen cases of such possession. The Capuchin was the last personage to enter Anna Ecklund's room on that morning of September 1, 1928.

Definitely, Father Theophilus Riesinger was no Fulton Sheen or Billy Graham in appearance. Nearing 60, he was still a strong, muscular man, in excellent physical condition from a lifetime of disciplined monastic living. With his venerable grey beard and crucifix tucked like a short-sword through the cincture of his brown Capuchin robes, he looked almost like some patriarch from the past. Compared to the others that morning, he was relaxed, almost calm.

At that time every candidate ordained to the priesthood received among other Orders, the Minor Order of Exorcist — "the power to place your hands upon those possessed and through the imposition of the hands, the grace of the Holy Ghost and the words of exorcism, you shall drive evil spirits out of the bodies of those possessed." The emphasis once attached to it remains in the ceremony. Other orders are, you might say, simply conferred. But at this point, in conferring the order of Exorcism, the consecrating Bishop turned to the congregation and entreated them to "pray, etc."

Though common in the early days of Christianity, it's a forgotten rite today — unfamiliar even to most Catholics. Few priests ever use it — and, nowadays, never without the full approval of superiors. Because of the sacrament of Baptism — a primary tenet of all Christian religions — and other rites, the Church feels that cases of true diabolic possession are exceedingly rare. Moreoever, it's a matter of policy that such cases are never made public.

The case of Anna Ecklund — undertaken in the utmost secrecy — is the exception. But then, what occurred in the affair of Anna Ecklund which began in secrecy was soon the talk of the whole area. As the difficult case progressed, parish after parish was enlisted to join in a crusade of prayer.

4

"IN THE Name of the Father and of the Son and of the Holy Spirit!"

The grey-bearded venerable Capuchin made the Sign of the Cross. The woman on the bed began to tremble as those present joined in the opening prayer of exorcism: the Litany of All Saints.

"Lord, have mercy."

"Christ, have mercy."

"Lord, have mercy."

"Christ, hear us."

"God, the Father of heaven —"

Anna Ecklund, growing more agitated, suddenly growled.

Or, rather, from somewhere inside her, the "growl" came. Never once, throughout the long exorcism, did her tongue or lips move. Now it was as if, to quote the observers, "a beast had awakened within her bowels." The sound "filled the room."

Father Theophilus raised his voice. "God, the Son, Redeemer of the world —"

Though surrounded by the taut, praying nuns, the quivering woman suddenly "disengaged herself " — quoting the official record — "and with lightning speed, was carried through the air." She "landed" above the doorway of the old-fashioned, high-ceilinged room "and clung there with tenacious grip."

If there were any skeptics present — and certainly in prior discussion of the case, a number of clergy had been highly dubious — *that* took care of them.

The Sisters shrieked — and stared at Anna Ecklund attached to the ceiling. For Father Theophilus, though, it was important that hysteria be stopped before it started.

"You must bring her down. And keep her down!"

They brought Anna Ecklund down — "with effort."

Once on the bed, with the trained nursing Sisters directing the procedure much as they would have for a violent case in a mental hospital, the woman gave a moan and sank into a heavy coma. She was to remain in that state for the rest of the exorcism, becoming unconscious each morning as the rite began, waking when the day's exhausting ordeal was done — remembering nothing.

A certain calm restored, Father Theophilus went back to his Litany.

At "God the Son, Redeemer of the world," "God the Holy Spirit," and "Holy Trinity, One God," the unconscious woman writhed and "a gnashing of teeth filled the room." With the three invocations to Mary, followed by "St. Michael the Archangel, pray for us," she subsided for the moment "as if struck by lightning."

Throughout the long and impressive litany — intoned in Latin, of course — her reactions varied as pleas went forth to the various heavenly powers. Mention of "Choirs" and "Holy Apostles" brought "muffled groaning." *"Ab insidiis diaboli"* — "From the snares of the devil" — caused Anna Ecklund's body to jump convulsively. "Through Thy Cross and Passion" brought "moaning and yelping."

All of which was only a "warm up" to the unearthly phenomena to come.

The exorcist's primary problem was to find out if one or more devils had taken possession of the woman. According to Church dogma, Satan can be made to speak, give answer, even to tell the truth — though, as the Father of Lies, he still remains expert at misleading and sidetracking. That is why the right choice of exorcist is so important.

Father Theophilus was a veteran. Before the first afternoon was over, he brought forth "voices" — a "howling as of a pack of beasts." To state that everyone, except the experienced exorcist, was terrified, is putting it literally.

Despite the closed windows, the nerve-racking howls grew in volume. People came on the run, out of their homes and from nearby fields, till there was a sizable crowd milling around the convent.

Farmers opined the screaming was of pigs being butchered, in the old-fashioned, knife-sticking manner. Businessmen thought

25

a nun had been murdered. A few instinctively guessed the truth.

It was the very thing the Church dreads. There was only one thing to do: admit that a case of exorcism was in progress and ask all people of good faith to pray for the tortured person.

Unfortunately from point of view of narrative, there was no "clinical analysis" intended of the case at Earling — no intention that it should ever become general knowledge. Those that were present were no chroniclers — and besides, they had their hands full. The Church authorities are never interested in the drama as such, merely in freeing the possessed member. Thus, the only available account shows no day-to-day "story": just the basic facts and incidents: certain passages of detailed and pertinent dialogue: in brief, the incredible, overall picture of the battle for a woman's soul.

Delineation of scenes was likewise of no account to the recorders — and, of course, they had no idea of how long the case was to continue. A passage of related dialogue might be spread over two days and interrupted constantly — by the bedlam of devils, by their "attacks" through the unconscious woman, and the like. There were overlappings, prayers upon prayers, periods of intense "resistance" when all the exorcist had for his labors were unearthly howlings, repulsive Satanic phenomena — and, at the day's end, exhaustion on the part of all concerned. Still in all, save for the fact that it is difficult to determine whether some of the more hair-raising incidents are of a few hours' duration, or prolonged through a couple of days, a fairly coherent picture emerges. The one point to keep in mind is that, even when the required information was forthcoming — sometimes after great perseverance, sometimes in a veritable flood — the "conversation" was repeatedly interrupted and not always in sequence.

In the initial stages, too, the effects on Anna Ecklund were frightening. To begin with, the woman's body became grotesquely distorted, bloating until neither the Sisters nor Father Steiger could bear the sight. It was necessary for Father Theophilus to explain again and again that Satan would use every device within his power to make them call the whole thing off. He advised those present to take turns at getting outside into the fresh air — advice they accepted gratefully.

For his own protection (and with permission of the Bishop) the exorcist carried a consecrated Host in a pyx on his breast. The others had been certain the devil could not remain in the presence of what Catholics believe to be the Actual Body and Blood of Christ, but the Capuchin set them straight.

"The devil approached Christ when He walked on earth, tempting and taunting Him. Now, as then, he is bold. But his outrages against the Host are limited."

Under Father Theophilus' drive, the intermittent roaring in Anna Ecklund became, with dramatic suddenness, a recognizable voice. Asked "in the Name of Jesus, the Crucified Savior" if one or more spirits were involved in the case of possession, a voice from somewhere within the woman's body made answer.

"There are many!"

There followed another prolonged period of ugly bellowing and howling from the mute lips of the unconscious woman. Henceforth it was to occur every day, "sometimes lasting for hours." A dozen nuns organized themselves into relays, so there was always a fresh group ready when Anna Ecklund needed them most.

And they *were* needed. For if the howling was unnerving, worse was to follow. The possessed woman began to froth, spit, vomit forth "unmentionable excrements" — as often as 20 times in a day. Though she was scarcely to eat throughout the incredible ordeal (and then only light foods, mostly liquids, in the evenings after exorcism) unbelievable quantities of obnoxious matter poured from her. Some of it resembled "vomited macaroni," some "chewed and sliced tobacco leaves." Towards the end, the outpourings were such as were "humanly impossible to lodge in a human body."

Time and again, Father Steiger and the horrified nuns were certain the woman was dying on their hands; and time and again, Father Theophilus had to plead with them not to panic. This, he said, was the possessing devil's counter-attack. As for Anna Ecklund dying, he assured them the devil could not go that far.

From his viewpoint, he was making real progress by then. And, frightened though they were, even the others recognized it. They could clearly discern a number of "voices" amid the bellowing and moaning.

It was soon apparent that two basic types of demons possessed Anna Ecklund. Devils from the realm of fallen angels seemed "more reserved." In the presence of the Blessed Sacrament, they "howled mournfully, like whipped dogs." Others — once the active souls of men on earth — were described as "bold and fearless." Once "raised," they caused the most violent excretions to come forth from the hapless woman — "as if they would desecrate the Sacred Host but were unable to."

Now, under the pressure of exorcism, the first possessing demon suddenly gave voice. Herewith from the records:

"In the Name of Jesus and His Most Blessed Mother, Mary the Incarnate, who crushes the serpent's head, tell me the truth! Who," thundered the old Capuchin, "is the leader or prince among you? What is your name?"

There came "a barking, as of a hound of hell." Then a "voice":

"Beelzebub!"

"Lucifer, the prince of devils?"

"Not the prince. But one of the leaders."

"A fallen angel?"

There was "a snapping of teeth," then the admission: "That is right!"

"One of those whose pride made him want to be like God?"

The barking again, then a pronounced sneering. "We hate Him still."

"Why did you rebel?"

The sneer and the snap of teeth again. "Look who has to ask!"

"Because Christ the Son was to take human form?"

A barking roar of "outrage."

"But you brought that about! You tempted Adam and Eve. You caused our fall, which in turn wrought our redemption!"

"That was later. Our testing was different than yours." A sudden pause, then carefully: "You're very interested in all this?"

"Yes."

"Then what about a deal? I will give you that knowledge, perhaps, if you promise to send her (the woman) away."

"And how would I know it was the truth?"

Convincingly: "You'll know!"

"You must know I'll never stop now until the woman is free."

"I know more than you, that's certain!" Beelzebub's pride was stung. "I have not lost any knowledge or intellect, remember!" Grudgingly: "You are hard to discourage, but this time you will not win."

It was too early for Father Theophilus to

be worried.

"Getting back to the point, why are you called Beelzebub if you are not the prince of devils?"

Insolently: "Keeping to the point, I don't have to answer that. My name is Beelzebub. That's enough for you to know."

"From point of influence and dignity, you must rank near Lucifer?"

No answer.

The next question was a superb stroke of spiritual swordsmanship, so to speak — a thrust at the enemy's weak point: pride.

"Or do you hail from the lower angels?"

"You imbecile! *I once belonged to the seraphic choir!*"

"What would you do if God made it possible for you to atone for your injustice to Him?"

"You *are* a fool! Don't you know your theology?"

"All right. How long have you been torturing the unfortunate woman?"

"Since her fourteenth year."

"How dared you enter an innocent girl? How could you enter?"

There was a burst of derisive laughter. "Wouldn't you like to know?"

"I command you, in the Name of the Crucified Christ —"

"Lay off it! I've had enough of that drivel."

"Then tell me. Why?"

"Her own father cursed us into her!"

"And why did you, Beelzebub, choose to take possession of her?"

"You talk foolishly. Don't you get your orders?"

"Then you are here at the command of Lucifer?"

"How else?"

As he was to do with the others, the Capuchin priest conversed with Beelzebub in English, German and Latin. The devil, like the others to follow, replied correctly in the tongue in which he was addressed. He was so language-perfect, in fact, that when Father Theophilus mispronounced the odd Latin word, Beelzebub shrieked corrections — and castigations.

"You pronounce it thus!" There followed the correct way, according to Beelzebub. "How'd you get through Latin, blockhead?"

Asked why the father of Anna Ecklund had cursed her, Beelzebub muttered inarticulately. The tiring Capuchin turned to the parish priest.

"What did he say?"

The stunned Father Steiger had missed it, too. They turned to the nuns. " 'She gave him no peace,' I think," one Sister volunteered.

"You lying little virgin!" Beelzebub howled. "Stick to the truth! I said: 'Leave me in peace.' Ask him yourself."

"I ask you this: is her father one of the devils within her now?"

There was a burst of "sneering laughter

mixed with malicious joy."

"He is!"

"Since when?"

"Since his damnation."

Demoniac laughter almost drowned out the strong voice of the exorcist. "I solemnly command, in the Name of the Crucified Savior of Nazareth, that you present the father of this woman and that he give me answer."

5

A DEEP rough voice completely filled the room terrorizing the nuns even more than the dialogue with Beelzebub. (After the first day or so, however, they both dreaded and expected the voices to become clearly intelligible.)

"Are you," asked the exorcist formally, "the father who cursed his own child?"

There was a defiant roar. "No!"

The exorcist, it is recorded, was momentarily startled. "Then who are you? I command you to give answer, to speak the truth."

"I am Judas!"

"Judas Iscariot? The former apostle?"

The answer was a "horribly prolonged" affirmative, howled in a bass voice so fearful that, this time, Father Steiger fled from the room — though most of the nuns stuck to their post.

The exorcism lost ground and was resumed with another session of spitting and vomiting that, in turn, settled down to a long-drawn battle of endurance that lasted for days. Like Beelzebub before him, however, Judas, too, was forced to give answer.

The recorded dialogue — as lengthy as with Beelzebub and as full of irrelevancies —

revealed that the chief mission of Judas was to bring Anna Ecklund to despair.

"Why?"

"To cause her to commit suicide. To make her hang herself."

"But you cannot?"

"We might have if you hadn't interfered."

"Might have?"

"She has free will." There was a stream of "shocking" curses; Judas' frustration was evident. When Father Theophilus interrupted, he raved anew over his mission. "She must get a rope. She must feel it around her neck!"

There was a "general howling" on the part of the unseen audience that made the nuns' flesh creep. It took another full day after this ecstatic orgy of agony before Father Theophilus got back to Judas again and the business of suicide.

"Is it true that everyone who commits suicide goes to hell?"

"I'd like that to be true. But it's not."

"Why not?"

The gist of Judas' answer was that, in many cases, the devils overdid their tempting, destroying the element of the victim's deliberate choice. The memory of being thus cheated caused another infernal moaning.

Father Theophilus, no doubt because of the central character of this conversation, questioned Judas about the betrayal of Christ.

Judas cursed horribly. "Don't talk about that!"

"Don't you regret committing the despicable deed?"

Another "terrible curse" — not given in the records — followed. "I said don't talk about that. I made my choice. Leave me alone."

The talk degenerated once more into "terrible cursing and raving," and more or less covers all that Judas had to reveal of interest. But it was far from the end of what was to come.

At about this stage, Lucifer — the prince — became manifest, though, from the accounts, he seemed to inject himself at will, sometimes silencing his subordinates, sometimes throwing the whole ritual into almost-reverse gear. At such times, "countless brats of devils" interrupted the exorcism "by their disagreeable and almost unendurable interferences."

Lucifer's presence was always dramatically marked — not by a smell of fire and brimstone, but by swarms of "avenging spirits," for instance, "filled with hatred and anger against all human beings." Lucifer boasted they were "powers of discord" — able to magnify small grievances into mountains, to set a parish against its pastor, brother against brother, man against wife.

The job of demons termed "principalities" — four, in particular, who declared they once had been "chained" in the river Euphrates — was to show "discord among nations." Obviously they had no particular concern with Anna Ecklund, except insofar as the devil used them to hold up the rite of exorcism.

Lucifer, throughout, showed himself master of retort and a wily tactician — his objective obviously to frighten the participants, delay the inquisition, exhaust the exorcist and thus prevent him from driving out his established forces.

During his presence, Anna Ecklund's face became so distorted that her features were unrecognizable. The "vilest of stenches — the odor of hell" filled the room, so that (with the expected exception of Father Theophilus) even the nursing nuns gagged and fled outside for air. Mrs. Ecklund's body, thin and emaciated, bloated up hideously, until the terrified Sisters thought it would burst.

The only response Father Theophilus had for these interrupting attacks was prolonged personal prayer mixed with persistent exorcism. Approaching again and again with a Relic of the Cross, and intoning the prescribed words: "Look on the wood of the Cross! Begone, Satan! Begone, all you powers of hell!" he time and again forced Lucifer into temporary retreat, leaving the exorcist free to do battle with the established devils.

Apparently, too, various parts of the rite affected Lucifer differently than the possessing demons. The ejaculation, *"A spiritu fornicationis, libera nos, Domine!"* — "From the spirit of fornication, Lord, deliver us!" evoked desperate "squirming" of the possessed woman's body. "Through Thy Cross and Passion," brought forth the by-now familiar moaning and yelping. The injunction, "I command you in the name of the Immaculate Conception, in the name of her who crushes the serpent's head," produced a sudden "languishing" of his activities. "He relaxed," says the account, "as one mortally stunned."

To a layman, Lucifer's status as resident is slightly confusing. Apparently, though, he was not a "possessing" spirit, but more of a visiting general. The impression is that abiding demons are localized in their activities, while he needs freedom of movement — to be "abroad."

"How else," he asked once, "am I to organize the Anti-Christ?"

When Father Theophilus inquired as to why he persisted in such a "useless" battle (presumably the battle of the ages — not the localized struggle over Anna Ecklund) Lucifer was unusually sardonic.

"Useless? It's a matter of viewpoint" — one that "limited minds" couldn't be expected to understand. The whole issue, Lucifer added, had begun "before the morning began," in accordance with "set laws."

"The morning?" Though all this sounds like telephone conversation, each hour supped tremendous energy from the exorcist, and he became slightly confused. "What morning?"

"What morning?" To Lucifer the priest's

mental block was calculated insult. "I was the Light of that morning! You clumsy creature of clay, do you not know who I am?"

To the analyst, this is a completely fascinating segment, terminated all too soon — though understandably enough. For the Church, this was no game — and the official account emphasizes that Father Theophilus had no wish to pursue such "unrelated" subjects, obviously designed to tantalize and exhaust him (and sap his energy). At times, the conversation logically veered into such channels; at other times, in a semi-hypnotic stupor of weakness, Father Theophilus simply was unable to keep from "drifting" with the current of conversation.

Unlike the special demons, Lucifer refused to talk much about his own particular past. He "refused" also to listen to the prayer beginning, "St. Michael the Archangel, defend us in the day of battle! Be our protection against the wickedness and snares of the devil" — recited at that time by the Catholic faithful after every Low Mass. Presumably its historic overtones rankled.

Lucifer's reaction to various sacramentals varied considerably. The sprinkling of Anna Ecklund's body with holy water, for instance, brought blood-curdling screams.

"Away with that abomination — that nauseating, burning dirt!"

A cross, made not of wood but papier-mache (as the surprised exorcist discovered later) brought derisive laughter. "If I remember correctly, He died, rather ignobly, on a wooden cross."

Side-tracking or otherwise, a remark like that was enough to snap Father Theophilus from his weariness.

"You were there?"

For his curiosity, he got two hours of bloodcurdling laughter. But the exorcist did win the admission that Christ's mysterious descent into hell (to free souls in Limbo, according to the Church) was a time of incredible torment. For the devils, not only was it a sign of the "last generation of man" — but Christ was accompanied by hordes of angels and the demons were commanded to adore Him.

The appearance of yet another crucifix (on the person of one of the nuns) evoked still more gleeful reminiscences on how He died.

Interestingly enough — in view of the emphasis the Catholic Church places on the vow of obedience among religious — Lucifer's principal attack seemed to be on superiors. Father Steiger's housekeeper (his sister) was never molested at the parish rectory. Nor were the nuns. The Mother Superior, however, took invisible blows that sometimes sent her staggering across the room. She and Father Steiger were objects of Satan's particular invective.

Extremely loquacious at times, he sometimes dwelt at length on his past relationship with mankind. Particularly interesting were his remarks on the pre-Christian era of the Greeks and Romans. They were "sensible enough" to want results, visible results, from their temple gods, Satan pointed out, and became highly-incensed because the Mother Superior mentally labelled that long-gone generation as being easily deceived.

"They weren't as naive as you, you old dark cloud! Read their writings!"

But didn't the heathens believe they could divine the future by probing entrails? Didn't they believe their heathen idols spoke?

Retorted Lucifer, with a roar of injured pride: "They *did* speak!" Then: "Your idiocy is unbelievable!" The inference in that remark is obvious: presumably he could as easily give voice through idols as through Anna Ecklund.

Lucifer adopted an injured air over the attitude of modern religionists. He challenged anyone to deny he had ever let down anyone open-minded enough to concede his power. Some he had showered with the kingdom of the world.

"But," queried Father Theophilus, "what of eternity?"

"Non ad rem!" Satan snapped, in Latin. "Not to the point!" He added peevishly: "You haven't the mind to argue an issue this big, anyway."

If he was curt with the exorcist, though, he unleashed torrents of contempt at Father Steiger. Never a day passed without him berating the pastor for permitting the exorcism at all — and the threats were very real to any priest.

Hadn't Father Steiger enjoyed the placid way life used to be in his parish? Lucifer inquired. Then why cause trouble. Finally he laid down his ultimatum. Either Father Steiger called the whole thing off, or "I'll incite the whole parish against you," presumably via the "avenging demons."

The pattern may seem absurdly clear from this viewpoint; but, actually, as Father Steiger admitted later, he was then laboring under tremendous doubts. And he was worried. What, he wondered, were people saying and thinking, especially after those days of horrible screaming from the convent?

The more the pastor brooded, the more his distaste for the whole affair grew. It seemed, somehow, grossly indecent. Away from the convent, he even began to doubt his own sanity. The thought struck him, finally, that anyone able to effect this sort of supernatural horror might even be a devil himself.

After yet another day's exorcism ended, he waited outside the rectory for the Capuchin's return, wondering if he should order Father Theophilus out of the parish entirely before the whole affair became a national scandal. West of Earling, the Iowa skyline was streaked with the afterglow of September sunset. Down the hard dirt roads, an empty truck rattled: some farmer, hauling wheat, was hurrying home. Father Steiger, staring unseeingly at the wheat stocks huddling in the stubble that stretched to the edge of the quiet little town, worked himself into anger.

Father Theophilus, returning wearily, managed a faint smile.

"After you've had your supper," Father Steiger began coldly, "I think we had better do some serious talking."

For Father Theophilus, eating was, by now, almost impossible. He turned his tired blue eyes on the man who had always been his lifelong friend.

"Father, think of that poor woman!"

"Now, look here! I have my own parishioners. . . ."

"Don't you see, Father? That is all he needs now, to win."

It was a critical moment in the case, but after some lengthy praying, Father Steiger thought he did discern the strategy. At least his decision could wait till he had attended to some piled-up parish business.

The next time he entered the convent room, Lucifer broke off his current subject to berate him worse than before.

"So you wouldn't have it the easy way? Then suffer!"

For Father Steiger, it was exactly what he needed. He stiffened. "You can't harm me!" he said, defying Lucifer. "I stand now under the protection of Christ Himself. . . ."

"I can't?" The devil was beside himself. "I've had better priests than you shot down on their own altars. *And I hung Him on a Cross!*"

The exorcist tried to intervene. "Leave the pastor alone! I am the one who fights you

— not he! Stop picking on him, now."

"He gave permission!" There was a burst of the sharper laughter, indicative of Lucifer's particular annoyance. "And he shall pay for it — on Friday!"

6

THE following Friday, as he was finishing breakfast at the rectory after Mass, there was an urgent sick-call for Father Steiger, the Earling pastor. The mother of a farmer-parishioner was seriously ill. The farmer's car perversely refused to start. Could Father Steiger take his own car? And could he please hurry?

Father Steiger's car was new — a surprise gift from his flock — and he knew every foot of the road. For the first time since he had ever rushed out to administer the Last Rites to the dying, he did not, however, hurry.

Returning along the hard dirt road, he drove even more slowly. Approaching a bridge near Earling, he was suddenly aware of a "black cloud" blotting out first the guard-rails, then the entire outline of the bridge. He jammed on the brakes. Even so, the car "hurled itself" towards the cloud.

A farmer, hearing the crash, hurriedly left his harvesting and came running. He found the car a shambles, the steering wheel smashed. Then he saw Father Steiger crawling out of the wreckage, white as a sheet and shaking.

The farmer got his own car and drove the priest to Earling, where the doctor found "some external bruises and a state of nervous excitement." Otherwise, Father Steiger was unhurt.

A stubborn Teuton at heart, the priest turned his steps towards the convent. The instant he entered Anna Ecklund's room, uproarious laughter upset the exorcism again.

"Rather proud of that new car, weren't you, boy? How do you like it now?"

As it turned out, the sympathetic (and quite prosperous) farmers of Earling were to buy Father Steiger a new car; but the devil kept raising the incident and promising "more fun."

It came — in rat-like gnawings in the night, slamming doors and sudden "movements" of his bed that brought him awake with the sweat burning on his skin. Nerves rubbed raw, and robbed of desperately-needed sleep, he finally resorted to reciting the "small office" of exorcism, which eventually stopped those disturbances.

Other priests — there were a number permitted to watch the exorcism — later reported similar noises and experiences. They, too, took to sleeping with holy water and stole nearby. (Some of them, it might be mentioned, were among those most skeptical in the initial stages of the Earling affair.)

Deriving but little satisfaction from all this — but keeping it up, nevertheless, for its fine psychological value — Lucifer suddenly opened a new attack. He threatened to disclose "rather embarrassing" details from out of the past lives of those taking active part in the exorcism. When Father Theophilus warned them to stand their ground, he proceeded to make good his threat.

"You remember, Sister" — this to one of the more reserved nuns, by name — "the summer you were eleven years old?"

The Sister was startled — and suddenly scarlet-faced.

"No need to be *that* embarrassed," said the devil smoothly. "Just leave and we can drop the whole incident."

Nuns don't get to be nuns, though, without learning a lot about courage and discipline.

"I had forgotten that!" whispered the stricken Sister. Then, with feminine defiance: "If you're going to bring up the sins of my childhood days, go ahead! Why don't you tell everyone those of my adult years?"

"Unfortunately," said Lucifer calmly, "what you have confessed, I have no way of knowing."

To the chroniclers, this was an "astonishing admission" — though it undoubtedly explains, at least in part, why the rubrics in the Roman ritual for exorcism demand a general confession beforehand on the part of all those involved in a case. It also explains why no one may participate in such a ritual without permission of the Bishop.

Thus committed, Satan began torturous

hours of "insinuating disclosures," sparing no one. A master of exquisite torment, he made perhaps the smoothest opening of any on his arch-irritation, Father Steiger.

"Ah, the good parish priest again! Too bad there's nothing more important to busy you. Well, since you're here again, I'm sure everyone will enjoy hearing tidbits from your saintly past."

"Be damned to you!" — or words to that effect — was Father Steiger's usual rejoinder. Under the circumstances, he could deliver the epithet without any fear of censure.

It wasn't so much what the devil disclosed, it was what he implied — though the record makes clear that Satan did know, with the exception of "sins confessed," all the human vanities, and weaknesses of those present. The strategy was to scandalize, shock and immobilize the group — and apparently it came close to succeeding.

Not for nothing, though, had Father Theophilus been given charge of the case.

Certain now that Lucifer was outdoing himself for a purpose much more important than the shielding of Beelzebub, Judas and scores of lesser spirits, the old Capuchin drew a new issue of weapons from his spiritual stockpile and concentrated everything on Lucifer in person.

The enemy yelled, howled, worked hideous physical phenomena — but stuck stubbornly to his position. During periods of stalemate, he and Father Theophilus crossed

48

swords verbally: the result is some of the most extraordinary dialogue in the whole case.

"When you know your time is limited," queried Father Theophilus, "why do you persist in your treachery and deceit?"

"Oh-ho! Ho-ho-ho!" Satan derived amusement from that one. "We've got our reasons, bright boy."

"If men realized that, it would be different for you."

"Why not tell them?" Satan broke into laughter, while more of the "terrible moaning" filled the room. "Since you missed the joke, blockhead, I was thinking of my friend Judas! Guess Who he had for his teacher!"

"But when time ends" — obviously Father Theophilus was trying his best to pursue a straight line — "you are damned to the pit forever?"

"A decided advantage. Unlike you," said Satan, apparently using the pronoun in the plural, "we have no illusions on that score. That was quite settled before earth emerged from its twilight."

"You mean darkness?"

"Not as of the night — of the morning. It was pretty."

"From your viewpoint? Or ours?"

"Any viewpoint," said Satan succinctly and, it seemed to the listeners, with "sudden infinite sadness."

"But God is all beauty! To you, too?"

"Non ad rem!" Lucifer was back to form. "That is precisely why beauty is our torment

— why we lust to destroy it."

"But you know you cannot!"

"We are limited," Satan admitted. "We cannot touch Him, true — except indirectly."

"Even then, you must know your time is set?"

Sardonic laughter. "Much better than you" — apparently in the plural again, and apparently with reference to men knowing the duration of their earthly lives.

"Do you know exactly when?"

"The year?"

"Yes."

There was a significant pause. Then:

"What kind of talk is this?" Satan asked peevishly. "Do you suppose we have access to that kind of knowledge?"

"Then you don't know?"

"I believe I mentioned before" — Lucifer seemed stung to sarcasm — "you haven't the mind to grasp this sort of thing at all. And," roared Satan, amid a "gnashing of rage," "your kind He had to favor! Above us!"

The exorcist was a model of persistence. "You're damned and you know it. You made the worst possible mess of your own chance for happiness — yet that is not enough. You cannot see others win where you have failed."

"Well put," said Satan politely. "Blockhead!"

"There is nothing good in you!" *That* wasn't a question, but it seemed to amuse Lucifer to flaunt his intellect. He swung over to his favorite topic — the Anti-Christ.

"It's a matter of measure — which you won't understand. A matter of 'his' vanity, of which you should have some slight knowledge. So, as time slows to die, it's perfectly reasonable that we must be active. There must come the time of the Anti-Christ. You have seen nothing to what will be seen then. His loss is our respite. Do you see that much, stupid?"

The only interpretation ever attached to this was that Satan's reference to "a matter of measure," etc., had to do with the theological explanation for the creation of human beings in the first place: to replace the fallen angels. But — and this speculation is anything *but* Catholic dogma — as long as the devils are adding to *their* numbers, the number of the elite must also grow. That would conceivably give Lucifer "reasonable" grounds for his ceaseless activities: every human soul lost to heaven would continue to offer him at least hope of prolonged "respite."

This seemingly friendly, exchange of rapport certainly fooled no one, least of all Father Theophilus. The stunt, he said, was as old as Eve: a cunning mixture of truth and deception, designed with Lucifer's ends in mind — not theirs. And nothing the devils said on "irrelevant" matters could be believed — not even the unhappy admission by Judas that he was the damned apostle. As far as the Church is concerned, it might, or might not, be so. They do not judge men's morals beyond the grave.

Lucifer remained very much to the fore for almost two solid weeks — by which time the untiring Capuchin's suspicions were verified. Even the others were aware now that, in the person of Anna Ecklund, two more powerful devils were entrenched. On them, the Capuchin was at last able to concentrate his fire.

They came forth amidst clouds of "dumb devils," more pestering than powerful, that caused a confusion of sounds but were easily driven away by the commands of the exorcist, only to return again and again — frustrating and wearying the exorcist.

By this time, in fact, Father Theophilus was on the verge of a physical breakdown. The case had become so long-drawn and critical that, in a move unprecedented in modern times, the pastor received permission to ask publicly for prayers, fasting and penance on the part of the local parishioners. Everyone in the vicinity of Earling knew that something very unusual was going on in their midst. Even the busy farmers flocked to morning Mass and evening devotions — and Father Theophilus went to the task with what strength he had left.

7

THE FIRST demon yielded, like the others, under the familiar prayers of exorcism. As in the case of Judas, the listeners could tell by his voice that he had once been a human being. The exorcist ordered him to reveal his name.

"Jacob."

"Which Jacob?"

"Her father!"

Father Theophilus Riesinger was anything but bashful in his probing. The record of exorcism simply condenses a hair-raising story of a life completely irreligious, coarse, brutal and "loathesomely unchaste," culminating in Jacob's repeated attempts to force his daughter, Anna, to commit incest with him.

"And she would not?"

Anna would not.

In fact, on the last occasion of her refusal, she threatened to tell her mother, the priest and everyone else what he wanted of her. The enraged Jacob "cursed her in her hearing — I willed the devils in hell to enter into her and drive her to orgies of abominations."

"How old was she then?"

"Fourteen."

"You — her own father —"

The exorcist was stopped with an unprecedented torrent of filth, spittle and excrement. That day he changed apparel four times, drove back the swarms of dumb devils, and kept forcing Jacob to answer.

Herewith excerpts from the dialogue between men and demons:

"After death, were you not freed from these lusts?"

"You are not freed after death. Only before."

"Then, before death, did you never once feel sorry for cursing her? Had you not one bit of unselfish love for your own child?"

Jacob made it clear he hated her more, with "a consuming torment" worse than any physical torment he had ever known on earth. The exorcist asked him why he hadn't repented even imperfectly, for fear of an eternity of torment. To that question he received an inarticulate growl.

"Speak clearly!" The priest fell back on his sacramentals again — the cross, holy water, lighted candles. The demon, Jacob, whined in such torment that — rather oddly, from this distance it evoked pity in some of the praying religious.

"Spare me these. I mocked them on earth, not knowing what power they have here — even as we have powers against you."

"Then, speak! Did you have no chance to repent?"

Jacob revealed that his death was not

sudden. Rather, he had even received the Sacrament of Anointing of the Sick.

"You received the Last Rites and still you were damned?"

Jacob, it turned out, had stayed in character to the last. Not only had he scoffed and mocked, he even found such solicitude good for laughs. But to keep a certain peace in the family, he consented to the rites. He added plaintively: "I did not believe I would die then, anyway."

"I am not clear on your condemnation. Was it for your refusal to repent?"

In a long-drawn explanation, Jacob conveyed the information that he might have been saved in spite of all — that he might, at the last moment, have received enough grace for repentance — save for the unforgivable crime of "giving" his child to the devils. That determined his damnation.

"And even yet you want to torture her, knowing what your own punishment is forever?"

"Till her end!" Jacob, in another world, was as unyielding as in this. His intensity of hate made the nuns tremble — literally.

"Satan commanded you to dwell in your own child?"

"I wished that, too. Satan rejoiced when I burned to enter into her."

The exorcist's voice stiffened. "The power of Christ Crucified and of the Blessed Trinity will force you from her forever — back into the pit where you belong!"

"No! No!" Jacob's "voice" rose, like that of an animal in death-agony. "Spare me that! You who call yourself a man of mercy — *no!*"

The man of mercy's sympathies lay elsewhere — with the unconscious woman who had begged so long for someone to help her; who lay now, helpless, dependent on him.

But there was still a fifth demon to come — one whose female falsetto voice had long been discernible alongside Jacob's. On her, Father Theophilus now concentrated the ritual of exorcism.

The most hateful of all in her replies — causing a hideous vomiting on the part of Anna Ecklund — she finally spat forth the admission that her name was Mina.

"Mina" meant nothing to anyone there. Father Theophilus pressed the question.

"Mina, the mistress of Jacob? You are damned because of your affair with him?"

Mina was not inclined to be as communicative about her personal life as the male demons. She muttered something about Jacob's wife being "still alive" (at the time of her affair).

Forced to talk, she revealed that, round for round, her life had been every bit as repulsive as Jacob's. It was, in fact, a classic of sodomy.

"This was the specific cause of your damnation?"

Mina had to admit worse — "unrepented" child murder.

"Whom did you kill?"

Bitterness filled Mina's voice — the one departure from her sizzling hate. "Little ones." No clarification of this was made.

"How many?"

"Three." Then, reluctantly: "No! Four."

"You were a Catholic?" From Beelzebub to Mina, Father Theophilus had to find out why they lost their souls. "Couldn't you have gone into Confession — made your peace with God?"

"You must repent — amend your life, too."

Mina went on to reveal flashes of a life as horribly sacrilegious as Jacob's. Unworthy Communions turned out to be the deciding cause of her damnation, then of her torment. The Host — as with Jacob — was the object of her burning hatred. The filth she brought forth from the body of Anna Ecklund was designed to desecrate.

These two demons, once human, were the most diabolically dedicated in their hatreds and obscenities.

For Father Theophilus there remained the last exhausting act of all exorcists — to drive these permanent, possessing devils from Anna Ecklund forever. Incredible as the drama seems today — though perhaps the average man is much more interested in the world beyond the physical than he might care to admit — you can scarcely repress a sense of comic relief to find, at this stage of the Earling affair, a "reluctance" on the part of the demons to be gone. Though obviously weakened, they begged not to be dispossessed — and their "groans of anguish" apparently had heart-rending effects on the witnesses.

"Spare us the tortures! Leave us in peace!"

To which Father Theophilus retorted: "Leave the woman in peace!"

"We are willing — but we *cannot*. Lucifer will not let us depart."

By now, the exorcist was working in a state of almost complete exhaustion (so much so, says the account, that he feared for his own life). He had been laboring without relief for 20 days — a period unprecedented in the history of the Catholic Church. In appearance, he had aged 20 years.

Faced with this last admission from the possessing demons, he made his decision. Though Father Steiger could no longer do without a solid night's sleep, though the alternating shifts of Sisters were so tired as to be moving half the time in a semi-stupor, he, Father Theophilus, was going to step up his efforts. So far, the exorcism had gone on from dawn each day, till dusk.

Now he would exorcise day *and night,* around the clock, till either he dropped or the demons departed.

The question of which it would be certainly worried the ecclesiastical authorities. Again, the Catholics of Earling and nearby parishes were urged to help, by constant prayer, fasting and vigils. Again, they flocked to the churches in droves. Father Steiger, after one good night's rest, returned, too.

The stepped-up exorcism had noticeable effect. Lucifer was less active personally, any of the four major devils could be called and mauled at will. Instead of the roaring and defiance, their voices were "pitiful and pleading" now.

"Spare us! Stop torturing us!"

"Then, go!"

"We cannot go!"

"Depart!"

"We will be driven back to hell."

"But you're in hell now!" You can almost hear the surprised note in the Capuchin's voice.

Apparently they weren't — at least literally. By their explanation, they were "of hell"; hell "is constantly with us"; but it was "tremendous relief" to be able to roam the earth, working hatred and malice, plotting and inciting the captivity of souls.

There were, these four disclosed, devils of many categories and ranks — imps of noonday, demons that travel only in darkness — all of them taking direction from leaders; the leaders, in turn, from *the* leader: the once-powerful, still-powerful, fallen Star of the Morning.

They were willing to talk, talk, talk — but not to depart.

For 72 hours without letup, they made an issue of their plight, pleading that it would be "more bearable" to be in another person, another place — anywhere than to be driven back down to the region of infernal torment, to give account of their ultimate failure.

But if Father Theophilus was teetering on the brink of complete collapse, the demons were likewise weakening rapidly, growing more apathetic by the hour, "docile and despairing." The end was near. Father Theophilus, advancing with the Cross, heard their cry of capitulation at last.

"No! Enough! We will go back!"

Father Theophilus, hard put to whisper, suspected a last and final deceit: a pretension on the part of the Big Four of leaving the possessed, then a stealthy return when the exorcism ended.

"In the Name of the Most Blessed Trinity, I command that you give me a sign of your leave-taking forever."

There was a last murmur of uneasiness, then a demand from Beelzebub as to the "sign."

It was almost nine o'clock in the evening.

Suddenly on the bed, the body of Anna Ecklund, inert for hours, "broke from the grip of her protectors." She stood upright, only her heels touching the covers — and for a horrifying moment, those present thought she would spring for the ceiling again.

But Father Theophilus knew victory when he saw it. From his worn Capuchin habit, the old priest drew forth his missionary's cross.

"Depart, you fiends of hell! I conjure

you, in the Name of Almighty God, in the Name of the Crucified Jesus of Nazareth, in the name of His purest mother, in the name of the Archangel Michael — begone, all you powers of Satan! The Lion of Juda reigns!''

The body of Anna Ecklund lost its stiffness. She fell back on the bed. "A piercing sound filled the room, causing all to tremble violently." In and over the sound came the "moan of many voices":

"Beelzebub! Judas! Jacob! Mina!" Then, as from a far distance, the voices wailing together: "Hell! Hell . . . hell . . . Beelzebub . . . Judas . . . Jacob . . . Mina . . ."

Suddenly in the convent at Earling, there was no longer any sound, except for the heavy breathing of the old Capuchin. He turned to the bed.

Anna Ecklund was resting "like a child of twelve."

She opened her eyes, then tried to smile.

"God bless you," Anna Ecklund said wearily.

Woman-like, the nuns began to weep. For a moment they were "scarcely aware" of the vile odor that filled the room again — "an unearthly, unbearable stench."

"Their parting gift," said Father Theophilus. "Open the windows. Air the convent. It is ended."

In Earling, Iowa, it was exactly 9 p.m., September 23, 1928 — 23 days from the time the Rite of Exorcism began.

Anna Ecklund went home in peace, to

"an untroubled life." No one, save the exorist and a handful of those concerned, ever knew her real name — and the few who did kept it well, under a silence as binding as that of the confessional.

How can anyone even begin to analyse the affair at Earling? Dangerously simplified, it appears as either the most fantastic psychosomatic phenomena ever surfaced in a suffering human being; or it is, simply, an insight into the drama of the ages. Some day, when man is done exploring basic physical laws — laws that govern the atom, for instance — he may get down to secrets more primary still: laws studied so far only by theologians and mystics. If and when he does, the case of Anna Ecklund will be a classic.

The incredible drama most certainly would never have become known at all, had it not been for its unforeseen violence and duration. The Catholic position on possession by the devil is outlined in every Catholic encyclopedia; but as far as the Church is concerned, publicity in actual cases merely alarms the faint-hearted and scrupulous and amuses the sophisticated.

On the Earling incident, the Church presumably made its own analysis and prepared to bury it. But the affair continued to create such a sensation, even beyond the borders of Iowa, that almost seven years later, on July 23, 1935, the Most Reverend Joseph F. Busch, Bishop of St. Cloud, Minn., placed the imprimatur on an approved summary of the case. This was an English translation, by the Rev. Celestine Kapsner, O.S.B., of St. John's Abbey, Collegeville, Minnesota, of an earlier account set down in German by the Rev. Carl Vogel. Everyone concerned was fully aware that the move was completely unprecedented. Other cases of exorcism — in Africa, Europe, China — have been *mentioned* — but never documented. The Earling case remains the only one on which even a semi-detailed account has even been made public.

Among the many who publicly testified to the authenticity of Father Kapsner's document was a highly-respected Milwaukee physician and surgeon, Dr. John Dundon, who declared Father Theophilus "a pious priest very gifted in a specialty which should command the patronage of the medical profession, rather than be allotted to the realm of superstition or neocromancy." It took a lot of courage for the doctor to make that public statement, but familiar with the facts, he felt he had to.

By this time, of course, Father Theophilus Riesinger had long since tucked his great crucifix back into his Capuchin robes and taken his leave of Earling. His opinion of the affair was that its intensity and duration marked it as a sort of "test case" on Satan's part; and he saw in it an ominous indication of things to come.

For all that, he lost none of his unshakeable faith in the ultimate triumph of good over evil, the gradual triumph of all that was fine in mankind over all that was base. Nor did he show any reluctance to spare himself in the overall battle — in fact, by 1935, his record of exorcism had climbed to 19, a figure probably unparalled in modern times.

In the later years of his life, he was in great demand for preaching quiet little missions in calm country parishes; and it is safe to assert that not one in ten thousand, even among Catholics, ever connected him with the affair at Earling.

When it came to sermons, he loved nothing better than to warm up by quoting St. Paul. "Brethren, we wrestle not against flesh and blood, but against principalities and the powers of darkness. . . ."

Grasping the hilt of his great crucifix and with his flowing white beard, he made quite a picture of the quaint, old-fashioned type of missionary — so much so that even the most sophisticated had to concede that old Father Theophilus certainly talked convincingly on the world, the flesh and the devil.

The Possession Problem

by Richard J. Woods, O.P.

Ed. Note: Fr. Richard J. Woods is a specialist both in the study of films and in the philosophy of religion. This article of his is reprinted from the Spring, 1973 issue of Chicago Studies, *a journal edited by the faculty of St. Mary of the Lake Seminary and the priests of the archdiocese of Chicago.*

WHEN the New York *Times* magazine section featured an article on the devil by Fr. Andrew Greeley (Feb. 4, 1973), it was abundantly clear that the subject of Satan was again relevant. A month earlier, Dr. Martin Marty had observed in the *Christian Century* (Jan. 10): "Yes, the devil is relevant as always: to explain what's wrong with the other guy, with your opponents, or with yourself, in case you don't want to take responsibility in the world."

Since 1966, when Ira Levin's *Rosemary's Baby* and Anton Szandor LaVey's *Church of Satan* were sprung on "secular" citizens, the devil has been making a striking comeback in the religious consciousness of American Christians (and others). The overwhelming success of William P. Blatty's obscenely pious novel, *The Exorcist,* testifies to the continuing fascination Satan exercised on our contemporaries. The film version, made with the active cooperation of several Jesuit priests and Chicago's Fr. John Nicola, the reported guru of U.S. demonologists, promises to reap even more from sowing demonic winds — especially cash benefits. It is not surprising that, according to Hollis Alpert (*World,* Feb. 14), Warner Brothers considers Pope Paul's recent statements about Satan and evil "a virtual endorsement of the film. 'Never underestimate the power of a publicity man,' said Howard Newman . . . in charge of publicity for the picture, [who] regards the Pope's remark as a considerable coup for his department."

Well he might. Since the days of D.W. Griffith, Hollywood has known only too well how to squeeze every drop of cash value from exuberant ecclesiastical endorsements of spectacular films, a trick developed to a peak of refinement by Cecil B. deMille, whose main contribution to cinematic religion was technicolor prurience. Occasionally a fiasco like *The Cardinal* appears, which is merely embarrassing. But Warner Brothers has invested a lot in the success of *The Exorcist* — not only six million dollars, but the talents of William Friedkin, who directed *The French Connection,* and actors of the caliber of Lee J. Cobb and Max von Sydow. (It is not known who is playing the demon.)

The only trouble, of course, is that the

Pope was not talking about *The Exorcist,* book or film; and it may be doubted whether the venerable Patriarch of the West would countenance a story about a little girl who masturbates with a crucifix. Be that as it may, Mr. Alpert blithely announces that *The Exorcist* is being made "with full Catholic approval."

Such statements would be merely comical if the situation were not more serious from a pastoral viewpoint. The problem with *The Exorcist* is not that it is bad, but that it is convincing, at least to the unwary. No doubt, Mr. Friedkin's notable talents as a realistic director will make the film more convincing than the book, even laced as it was with scholarly (if frequently twisted) references. Further, films in themselves tend to be more realistic than novels — a fact duly acknowledged in the transformation of the *Index of Forbidden Books* into the National Catholic Office for Motion Pictures.

A PASTORAL PROBLEM

As a student and teacher of media, a reviewer and sometime film-maker, I am not particularly averse to film art nor in favor of censorship, especially prior restraint. I am, however, opposed to deliberate distortion of facts, whether for the sake of dramatic interest or salesmanship, *á là* Warner Brothers. *The Exorcist* case is particularly serious, not only for these moral lapses — classified best, perhaps under "truth in advertising" — but because of the effect both the book and the film are having on a growing number of impressionable people.

The current heyday of diabolism is reaping much more than money; it is harvesting, or at least catalyzing, a whirlwind of spiritual and psychological disorders of frequently tragic consequences. A truly pastoral problem is in the making, whether or not it amounts to a "crisis" situation in other than individual lives. It is, simply, the problem of personal evil experienced as demonic possession, coupled with a desire, if not demand, for exorcism. The difficulty is compounded by many factors, not least of which is the official attitude of benign neglect toward exorcism in the Roman Catholic Church and a general skepticism regarding the devil, possession and exorcism.

What I intend to explore in the following article is the growing incidence of possession cases and exorcisms; their possible causes, both natural and supernatural; their consequences for mental and spiritual well-being; and, lastly the significance of the new emphasis on possession and exorcism for the Church's teaching and pastoral ministry. The perspective is that of pastoral theology and the philosophy of religion — not of film or literary criticism, although the peculiar nature of the recent possession-mania is that it thrives on the media, and so warrants some consideration of this factor. In particular, I am writing as a minister who has found himself with fourteen such cases referred to him in less than nine months, about half of them traceable to *The Exorcist*. Ministers and pastors as well as psychiatrists have informed me that in their own experience, the number of such cases is rising. As might be expected, so is that of amateur exorcisms. Given the "success" of the book, we can expect that following the release of the filmed version of *The Exorcist,* there will be a jump in the number of alleged possessions unmatched since 1692. And a good many of the clergy, and possibly doctors and psychiatrists, are likely to be about as prepared for the event as were the good people of Salem. *The Exorcist* is not, of course, the cause of all this; it is itself a symptom of a spiritual agitation in Western society that began long before 1966. The possession problem is the manifestation of spiritual disintegration, not the least danger of which is the emergence of a secret cult of the devil in the midst of the Church itself.

POSSESSION, PSEUDO-POSSESSION, EXORCISM

Possession is undoubtedly the rarest of all spiritual phenomena in Western religions, although it has always been present in some form, as T.K. Oesterreich adequately demonstrated in 1921 (T.K. Oesterreich, *Possession: Demoniacal and Other,* New Hyde Park, New York: University Books ed., 1966). Demonic possession is but one variety of possession, perhaps the rarest of all. Indeed, some students — for instance, Jean Lhermite (*True and False Possession,* New York: Hawthorn Books, 1963) — doubt that any genuine cases of demonic possession exist outside the New Testament accounts. Some scholars, such as Oesterreich, deny the reality of even the scriptural cases — not that they were possession states, but that a demon was responsible.

Recent experiences within the Christian fold seem to indicate, conversely, that possession, like miracles and charisms, may well be present and increasing. Consequently, it is not surprising that along with the growth of pentecostal groups, the charismatic renewal in the Catholic Church, the popular healing demonstrations of Kathryn Kuhlman and others, the increasing practice of lay exorcism, the publication of a new Anglican exorcism ritual two years after the rank of exorcist was dropped from Roman Catholic ordinations, the Pope's statements, the impact of *The Exorcist,* etc., a general sense of supernatural bewilderment has developed. The confusion has hardly been diminished by sibling controversies among right-wing Christian sects, who are seriously divided over the issue of tongue-speaking and other charisms. That popular writers in the Jesus movement, such as Hal Lindsey, can doubt the validity of glossolalia but accept possession, exorcism, etc., seems to give the devil a little more than his due. In general, nonpentecostal fundamentalist Christians seem likewise content to accept biblical testimony regarding New Testament cases of tongues, miracles, possessions, etc., but nothing thereafter, despite the seeming identity of the phenomena. Modern cases of such paranormal events are simply attributed to the devil, since they cannot come from God. The Catholic tradition has regarded such manifestations with caution, refusing to grant them divine or diabolical status *a priori,* nor without first ascertaining that they were not of natural origin; but it has generally adhered to the reality of post-Apostolic miracles. And although the demythologizing tendency of recent biblical criticism and the adoption of the scientific worldview has given many Catholics a strong sense of skepticism regarding the supernatural, the almost simultaneous eruption of the charismatic movement, complete with glossolalia, faith-healing, prophecies and poltergeists has reintroduced supernaturalism among adherents of the Old Faith.

POSSESSION AND PSEUDO-POSSESSION

What is evident in all of this is that a new sense of the supernatural, however confused, has emerged in the Christian community as a whole within recent years, much as Peter Berger has divined in *A Rumor of Angels.* But interest in the supernatural obviously extends beyond the borders of the Christian fold, as the wave of occultism flows on and the oriental and mystical sects flourish. And in the wake of the crisis mentality of the recent past, tenderized by emergencies such as the war in Vietnam as well as controversies ranging from abortion to papal infallibility, the new supernaturalism understandably surfaces in sometimes bizarre and pathological episodes such as possession and (especially) pseudo-possession.

In general, possession is experienced as an "invasion" of one's body by an alien, conscious personality which displaces the conscious personality (ego) of the victim. A state of complete or partial amnesia usually follows the phenomenon of possession. From a psychological viewpoint, this indicates that (in certain cases at least), there are not two real personal egos in conflict for control of one body, but that a fragmentation of the unified consciousness of one person has occurred. Oesterreich was not sure enough of this theory to embrace it as an explanation, nor did he consider possession to be a form of hysteria, since the dissociation of consciousness was the *only* symptom hysteria and possession appeared to share in all cases. Since 1921, however (as William Blatty seems unaware), studies of possession and trance states made with the aid of electroencephalographic and other instruments indicate that most possession cases are a variety of hysterical attacks or psychomotor epilepsy. It remains true, following Oesterreich, that as a species of what is now called "altered states of consciousness," possession states can be voluntary or involuntary, pathological or beneficial, dreaded or welcomed. A great many alleged possession states, however, are true schizophrenic reactions, a fragmentation of normal consciousness accompanied by amnesia and apparently, on occasion, paranormal phenomena. Such a state is theologically termed pseudo-possession, but need not imply deliberate fraud.

Regardless of whether the possession state is normal or abnormal, real or "pseudo," the possessed persons typically attribute their state to the presence of any one or several of a variety of spiritual beings — gods, such as the Vouduan *Loa;* ghosts, such as the spirits of the dead who allegedly speak through trance mediums; living persons and sometimes even animals; and demons, including the devil himself, although this is a notion devoid of any scriptural basis whatever. God, too, is sometimes believed to possess persons. Even in Christianity, tongue-speaking or glossolalia is interpreted as the Holy Spirit praying through the believers (although Paul seems to indicate in I Cor. 13:1 that even angels may thus possess). True prophecy, as the Nicene Creed affirms, is the Holy Spirit speaking through the prophets. However, neither the Father nor Jesus possess the believing Christian — although, of course, the Holy Spirit is the Spirit of the Father and Son, as the Creed also professes.

Most careful studies of possession as well as tongue-speaking (especially William J. Samarin, *Tongues of Men and Angels,* New York: Macmillan, 1972 and John P. Kildahl, *The Psychology of Speaking in Tongues,* New York: Harper and Row, 1972) conclude that originally these are not supernatural phenomena, but varieties of psychological abilities. There are, nonetheless, sound theological and even anthropological reasons for refusing to categorize *all* possession states within the scope of natural abilities.

THE NEW TESTAMENT

Demonic possession and other forms of spirit possession, although totally absent from the Old Testament, were clearly acknowledged in Egypt, Babylonia, and Persia from the earliest times. By the New Testament period, and in other contemporary accounts such as Josephus' *Antiquities,* possession and exorcism were recorded almost matter-of-factly, although with some interest. In the New Testament, not only do Jesus and His disciples cast out demons, but other Jewish exorcists also do so, using Jesus' name as their authority (Mk. 9:38 and Acts 19:73). Characteristic of Jesus' exorcisms is the simple brevity of His command to the demon to depart, in contrast to the lengthy conjurations and even fumigations of His pagan contemporaries. Significantly, Jesus is never called "exorcist," and the word "to exorcise" (*exorkizein*) is not used in this sense in the Bible. (References: Mt. 7:28-33, 17:14-21; Mk. 1:23-27, 3:22ff, 5:2-10, 9:17-27, 12:24ff, 43ff; Lk. 8:26-39, 9:35-45, 13:10-13; Jn. 9:44-45; Acts 19:13-16.) It is also significant that Jesus' authority to cast out demons is specifically transmitted to His disciples (Mk. 6:7, 13; 16:17-18; Acts 5:16,

16:16-18, 18:7, 19:12).

In New Testament usage the devil, Satan, does not possess. Only demons are exorcized, although they are apparently the agents of Satan (Mt. 12:26; Mk. 3:23-26), and when they are cast out Satan is also defeated. The word used to designate the possessing spirits is not the Greek *daimon,* which appears only once in scripture (Mt. 8:31), but *daimonion,* a term possibly indicating contempt. (In Greek usage, a *daimon,* could be either good or evil; a *daimonion,* "divinity," was a lesser being, apparently, which in New Testament usage was uniformly malicious). The *daimonia* are indeed contemptible and hardly of the stature of fallen angels. They more nearly resemble the vicious and even stupid entities modern occultists call "elementals." They cause illness and suffering, both physical and mental, but they do not appear to tempt, the prerogative characteristic of Satan. Their principal function seems to be to afflict, and in this they are manifestly Satan's servants, who is the "father of lies and a murderer from the beginning" (Jn. 8:44). A parallel situation can be found in certain psychotic disorders in which the victim claims to be controlled and tormented by "spirit voices" which often lead to severe depression, paranoia and suicidal tendencies. While it is groundless to affirm that all such people are possessed by unclean spirits, I would not rule out the possibility that some are actually so afflicted. As Fr. Nicola has suggested, many inmates of mental institutions may be more in need of spiritual healing than psychotherapy. On the other hand, a good many people who demand the services of an exorcist are more likely to be in greater need of a psychiatrist.

Odd as it seems, then, we need not ascribe possession to the devil, nor in every case even to demons. It is not even absolutely necessary to believe in the devil (or for that matter, in God) to believe in demonic possession. (Incidentally, there is only *one* devil in scripture, Satan as he is most frequently called and sometimes Beelezebub, but *never* Lucifer, a title that seems reserved for Christ — see 2 Pet. 1:19 and Rev. 2:28). Nevertheless, belief in the existence of the devil is certainly warranted by the New Testament, however that existence is conceived; Satan is mentioned by name in every book except the second and third Epistles of John. And although the devil is not mentioned in any of the creeds, the early Fathers, as well as the Doctors of later centuries, were unanimous in recognizing his existence, and it was explicitly spelled out by three Church Councils — the Fourth Lateran Council, the Council of Trent, and the First Vatican Council. It is one thing to believe that the devil exists, however, and another to believe it according to the mind of the New Testament and the Church. *Over*-belief in the power of Satan or demons, or even accepting as Christian teaching the myths of the devil that sprang up over a thousand-year period of Jewish and Christian speculation, is (as

Aquinas realized) a covert kind of devil-worship, and from a psychological and spiritual viewpoint more destructive than skepticism.

Thus, even though the term "diabolical possession" is not scripturally accurate, it is theologically sound to recognize as Christ did, the Satanic presence directing demonic seizures, even those we recognize as false possessions but are believed by their victims to be genuine. Obsessions with the *idea* of the devil are no less a Satanic attack insofar as they create spiritual and even mental disorders. Demonic possession, then, can include both true possession (which is extremely rare if it actually exists) and other pathological disorders, that is, possession states that are destructive of health or sanity.

SIGNS OF POSSESSION

According to Oesterreich, the physical signs of possession are changes in the facial features, voice and character of the possessed person, accompanied by powerful motor movements. The *Roman Ritual* specifies the psychological signs of knowing or speaking strange languages (glossolalia or xenoglossy) and knowing hidden or future events. Since the seventeenth century, however, theologians, following the Jesuit, Thyraüs, have held that not even these signs are decisive for determining genuine cases of demonic possession, since all of them can be accounted for by other factors. Further, for the last seventy years, the advances in parapsychology have been recognized by the Church as weakening the force of the psychological indications even Thyraüs held to be indicative. Thus, the Church demands that the final judgment be made only with expert consultation (which today would necessarily include medical, psychiatric and parapsychological tests) and after a careful consideration of the evidence as a whole. Importantly, the *Ritual* prescribes that a priest called to investigate a claim of possession "should not believe too readily that a person is possessed by an evil spirit; but he ought to ascertain the signs by which a person possessed can be distinguished from one who is suffering from melancholy or some other illness." Despite the seventeenth-century language, this caution has resulted from the Church's extensive experience with pseudo-possession. One of the earliest such *caveats* appeared in the *Acts* of the National Synod of Rheims in 1583, at a time the witchcraft mania was raging: "Before the priest undertakes an exorcism he ought diligently to inquire into the life of the possessed, into his condition, health, and other circumstances: and should talk them over with wise, prudent and instructed people, since the too credulous are often deceived, and melancholics, lunatics, and persons bewitched often declare themselves to be possessed and tormented by the devil: and these people nevertheless are more in need of a doctor than an exorcist."

There are times, such as the early seventeenth century and as late as 1692 in America, when the belief in possession seems particularly epidemic, a situation most sociologists and psychologists locate in the stresses of the personal and social life of people caught up in an uncertain era. The resort to exorcism in such cases has proved not only to have been useless but damaging; since the causes are often other than spiritual, the symptoms soon reappear, if they abate at all, as was the cause in Salem. When exorcism fails, the likelihood of despondency is enormous. Further, the dramatic nature of public exorcisms in particular adds fuel to the fires of social mania, such as those that racked Europe for over two centuries. Imprudent exorcisms increase rather than decrease the spiritual and mental damage of demonomania. Public exorcisms were forbidden for this reason by Cardinal Mazarin following the tragic events at Loudun in the mid-seventeenth century.

THE ROOTS OF POSSESSION

In our own times, when witchcraft — black, white and gray — has returned in force and even Satanism is rumored far and near, the four-hundred-year-old warning of the Synod of Rheims is still appropriate; for occultism can easily lead sensitive and suggestible persons into bizarre beliefs, including that of their own possession, against all evidence to the contrary. But pseudo-possession fattens on much more than occultism; both ardent and lax Christians who abhor or shrink from the sight of a ouija board often find themselves plagued by the same obsession as do the unwary occultists — and, it seems to me, for the same reason: they are attributing to a mere game (or whatever) a power it simply does not have. Such persons invest the object of their awe or fear with the energy of their own emotions, thus initiating the process of the self-fulfilling prophecy. The essence of idolatry is not the worship of idols, but attributing powers that properly belong to God (or even our own spirits) to demons or mere things, and then revering the objects as if they had such power. Thus, even Christians who find in Satan the subject of persistent fears and a target of their unceasing crusade, or who damn every occult foible as a tool of hell, are themselves falling prey to idolatry.

The ground is tilled for such aberrations by the failure to consider the symbols and even the real experience of evil in a truly Christian manner — that is, not taking them *too* seriously. A morbid interest in the devil or occultism, whether pro or con, is an open invitation to obsession and even possession.

Most cases of pseudo-possession appear to result from the interiorization (introjection) of external conflicts (public or private) which, because they cannot be ignored or simply accepted for what they are, become perceptible consciously as the presence of an evil spirit. A more serious and difficult situation arises when inner tension between a person's conscious self-image and his more or less unconscious awareness of guilt, fear, or desires leads to an externalization (projection) of the latter as an alien, conscious form. This type of pseudo-possession, in which a person is actually haunted by his own inner demons, is far more insidious and destructive than the introjection of social stresses, for it represents a fragmentation of the personality, a rejection of that part of the self for which one refuses to admit responsibility. The resulting, persistent "temptation," obscene suggestions, threats and accusations emanating from the "evil spirits" thus created intensify to the degree that the "possessed" person continues to deny the real identity of his demons. It is, as Dr. Marty insisted, much easier psychologically to blame the hideous wreckage of our lives on some devil than to put the blame where it belongs, on us. Perhaps we are afraid to accept responsibility because we lack the sense of adequacy and achievement that constitutes authority. How *can* we be responsible for events — e.g., inflation, the Vietnam war, the energy crisis, etc. — over which we have no direct control? And thus, we are led to excuse ourselves, but at the cost of introducing more demons into the world.

Traditionally, the causes offered to explain genuine possession are no less numerous than those for pseudo-possession, although much less convincing. Despite the fact that the New Testament is reserved to the point of silence about the cause of demonic possession, subsequent theologians have suggested everything from eating unblessed food to being hexed by witches (Salem) or cursed by someone. (Curses, like hexes, are feared not for spiritual but for magical reasons; likewise, possession cases increase in proportion to the emphasis placed on magic in a society. Curses are believed to work almost *ex opere operato,* implying that the "correct" words have a coercive effect even on God.) Some theologians, such as Msgr. L. Cristiani, maintain that possessions occur by God's will, for by them an incredulous world is taught to believe in His power, which is made manifest in the exorcism rite. Others seem to think that possessions result from the devil's envious hatred of men, especially saints, such as John Vianney, whom Satan will persecute (obsess) if he cannot possess them. Fundamentalists of all stripes, beginning perhaps with the incidents at Salem, find dabbling or delving in the occult a ready invitation to the devil to set up his house. (For further discussion, see Richard Woods, *The Devil,* Chicago: Thomas More Association, 1973.)

In short, there are so many explanations for demonic possession that none of them can be considered any more convincing than the others. The pastoral problem is not determining causes, however, but providing remedies, whether for genuine possession (if such a thing exists) and also for pseudo-possession (which certainly does exist). The latter does *not* call for a pseudo-exorcism, however, for reasons mentioned above, but rather for pastoral counselling and the ministry of healing. It was not without cause that the Church suspended priests who performed unauthorized exorcisms.

THE MINISTRY OF DELIVERANCE

Spiritual counselling is not a task to be undertaken lightly when the problem is as complex and profound as that of possession or pseudo-possession. So real is the feeling of possession, that the gruff or frivolous brush-off many perplexed "demoniacs" receive from busy pastors can result in a true crisis of faith, in which the sufferer's undeniable experience and hope for understanding assistance override his trust in the judgment of a skeptical and unimpressed minister. Nor, on the other hand, is an immediate attempt at exorcism the answer, despite the increasing incidence of such attempts by clergy and laymen.

What is called for in the case of the "introjected-conflict" pseudo-possession is a patient process of Christian *education*. By this, I mean an interpretation of the Christian attitude toward evil, particularly as based on Jesus' emphasis on non-resistance and deliberate acceptance of unmerited suffering. This is not spiritual masochism, but a realistic approach to the inescapable fact of evil in our lives, which we cannot overcome by denying it, but only by facing it, day by day. *Confession,* the humble acknowledgement of failure and sinfulness, is not only the most effective way of coming to grips with our own inner demons and outer conflicts, it is the necessary condition for appropriating God's forgiveness in order to be enabled to concentrate on the gracious, good and beautiful elements in every human person and in life itself. Thus, with pseudo-demoniacs, their awareness of guilt, even if exaggerated, should not simply be dismissed, but rather surpassed by an emphasis, first, on God's loving forgiveness, and then on their need to cultivate an attitude of loving trust, hope and honesty together with an effective willingness to forgive others. The real and basic goodness of people and the natural world should be constantly affirmed and demonstrated, to offset the pseudo-demoniac's hyper-sensitivity to the excesses of cruelty, lust, selfishness and greed that seem to be proliferating in contemporary society. A celebrative attitude toward life, a sincere enjoyment of fun and festivity, will more effectively dispel the gloomy mists of psychological and spiritual depression and obsession than will all the compulsory prayers of a lifetime.

The second variety of pseudo-possession described above presents far more difficult problems for effective spiritual counselling and possibly (though not necessarily) psychotherapy. For when the roots of the disorder are buried in the repressed depths of the spirit, the threat of true schizophrenia is grave. In his valuable study, *Occult Phenomena in the Light of Theology* (Westminster, Md.: Newman Press, 1957), Fr. Alois Wiesinger cites many cases of unconscious spiritual or psychic conflict resulting in a total disintegration. Conversely, it is a common occurrence for schizophrenics to hear accusing or threatening voices; the belief that an evil spirit is in possession of one's mind is thus practically indistinguishable from the paranoid delusions of true insanity. A spiritually naive psychiatrist will probably interpret all such symptoms identically. Nevertheless, psychiatry may represent the only immediate help for a severe "projected-conflict" pseudo-possession because of the complexity and depth of this kind of spiritual crisis. In a very real sense, psychotherapy is a type of exorcism. Often, however, because of the stigma attached to psychoanalysis and the cost, people who can benefit from the attention of a psychiatrist are reluctant to seek his aid, even if he is a Catholic. In such cases, the pastoral counsellor, if possible in consultation with a psychiatrist, may be able to assist the pseudo-demoniac gradually to confront his inner demons — the fears, anxieties, frustrations and desires which have assumed a kind of independent reality. It is useless to deny the existence of these "demons," at least initially, but it is possible to ignore them to some extent. A refusal to give them any unnecessary attention but to address the underlying spiritual problems can gradually starve the "evil spirits," depriving them of the emotional energy on which they subsist. Pathological psychological problems should, however, be referred to a therapist.

Spiritual healing, especially in community prayer service in which the participants pray over and for the afflicted person, may be an effective "therapy" for the pseudo-demoniac, and if such a group can be found, a real deliverance can likely be secured in simpler cases. But despite the power of faith and prayer, the same caution must be taken with such meetings as with public exorcisms. Unbalanced individuals often thrive on attention, and can even feign signs of possession, consciously or not — a situation which has occurred many times in the history of the Church. On the other hand, suggestible members of the group may also succumb to the forceful influence of the obsession. Because it is a kind of hysteria, pseudo-possession can be highly contagious. Consequently, a prayergroup should be carefully instructed before attempting a spiritual healing for a supposedly possessed person.

Spiritual healing is effective according to the measure of faith of the healers and the healed, as Jesus plainly taught. Consequently, an increasing incidence of spiritual disorders, such as the two types of pseudo-possession mentioned above presents a clear challenge to the *whole* Church to grow in faith. The experience of evil is not primarily an individual event in the Christian life, but a social reality, and the means of redressing evil are likewise social. The individual is never alone, but one of the most overwhelming temptations suggested to obsessed persons by their "voices" is that no one can help them. The solidarity of the members of the Christian community should be openly manifest in such cases, and expressed in both direct and indirect ways. Paul has directed us to bear one another's burdens; the individual under spiritual attack, whether from his own or possibly very real demons should never be allowed to feel separate from the love of God made visible in the living community of believers.

Regarding true demonic seizure, a sincere grasp of the meaning of the Christian scriptures and historical experience cannot preclude the possibility of possession, no matter how unlikely. The recent report of the ecumenical commission convened by the Bishop of Exeter and its proposed exorcism ritual indicate that the real possibility of such psychic attacks is still being taken seriously (*Exorcism*, ed. by Dom Robert Petitpierre, O.S.B., London: SPCK, 1972). But like the old Roman Ritual exorcism, the Anglican rite carries the instruction that in a case of suspected possession, an experienced minister be summoned to investigate. Amateur exorcisms are extraordinarily foolish and capable of causing immense spiritual harm and mental injury. Moreoever, the Christian struggle against the Principalities and Powers that continue to rule this world of darkness is not a matter of theatrical heroics such as Blatty celebrates in *The Exorcist*. The combat is waged by the Church of Christ; it is a common effort, not a hand-to-hand conflict of individuals. Individualism in the spiritual life is a Christian contradiction — and perhaps the greatest expression of such individualism is the egocentric entrapment of the possession mania. The wages of such individualism is spiritual death — psychological isolation in this life and eternal alienation in the next; hell is utter loneliness, the antithesis of the communal solidarity of love Christians call heaven.

THE MYSTERY OF EVIL

In *The Exorcist,* the terrible struggle against the "demon" results in no particular triumph for the Christian community. Two priests die and the victim's mother finds herself able to believe in the reality of the devil, but not of God. Unwittingly, I think, Blatty has here pointed out that where faith is lacking, exorcism need not increase it and, as well, the grip of Satan on the mind may actually be strengthened. So overwhelming seems the power of the demon, that even the Church's ministers appear helpless to overcome it, and God does not seem much interested in the whole affair. Thus, even *The Exorcist* teaches us that too much emphasis placed on the reality of occult forces or demons only serves to reinforce the fascination such ideas have on the credulous. Otherwise well-intentioned Christians who have become outspoken opponents of all forms of occultism and never tire of preaching the power of the devil in today's world are as much the victims of "occult bondage" as the people they castigate. The recent "anti-Satan" handbooks of Evangelists Hal Lindsey *(Satan Is Alive and Well on Planet Earth)* and Mike Warnke *(The Satan Seller),* like Arthur Lyon's *The Second Coming* and *The Exorcist,* too, along with its imitators, constantly reinforce the very forces they profess to oppose. And that is idolatrous.

Seven hundred years ago, St. Thomas Aquinas observed in his *Summa Theologiae* that the sin of idolatry consists of giving worship to God in an undue manner, which he calls superstition (I-II, Q. 92, a. 2). Idolatry also consists in giving the honor proper to God to creatures *(ibid.),* which, if such creatures are demons or the devil, is demonolatry. It is not beyond possibility that in overestimating the power and activity of the demonic in the world, Christians are actually giving credit where it is definitely not due. To attribute everything adverse to the devil is likewise superstitious. Yet that is a tempting possibility for people caught up in the throes of a disintegrating social system such as those of the tenth century, the fourteenth and during the great wars of religion in the sixteenth and seventeenth centuries, when hundreds of thousands of innocent victims went to the scaffold or the stake, having been accused and sometimes even believing themselves to be witches. (Some were, but the vast majority of those executed were undoubtedly innocent both in Europe and among the fifty persons hanged in the American Colonies at that time.) Likewise, cases of possession proliferated during these very times, and public exorcisms were common, until abuses warranted their suppression. In this twilight of the second millenium, our own epoch is hardly superior to the past in terms of moral degradation, war and civil strife. We should not be too surprised, then, that instances of possession and demands for exorcisms abound. But any sensitivity to the past mistakes of the Christian community should alert us to the fatal trap of succumbing to the devil-mania again. Nothing could be more pleasing to Satan than to see Christians neglecting their primary work — the creation of a Christian social order — to devote themselves to witch-hunts and public exorcisms.

From a pastoral perspective, counselling problems involving occult phenomena, including possession, are magnified by the likelihood that too much emphasis on the reality of power of occult forces or demons will reinforce the obsession which has led to the problem, whereas too great a de-emphasis will undercut the counselee's confidence in the ability of the counselor to grasp the situation. Traditional Christian approaches to the mystery of evil and spiritual affliction, whether obsession or possession, indicate the possibility of maintaining a necessary and delicate balance between overestimation and underestimation of psychic forces and the careful employment of methods such as exorcism. The devil's cleverest wile is not to persuade us that he does not exist, but that he does not exist where he really is at work. The devil's chief area of interest has always been the world, the social sphere — institutions and corporations, governments, mass movements and factions. His choice weapons are war, disease, famine, hatred and ignorance. Let us address ourselves to these, and we will not mistake the mystery of evil for the psychological manifestations of these situations in the life of individuals already made fearful by the seeming approach of Armageddon. What the world needs now is not the cultivation of fear nor even the politics of joy, but the witness of love and justice, truth and peace.

The Exorcism Rite and the Roman Ritual

THE little-used rite of exorcism contains few extraordinary or magical elements. Priests familiar with it stress that the rite's effectiveness stems from the intention of the Church to pray for an afflicted person and not from pronouncing certain words or making special signs.

Introductory material to the rite in the Roman Ritual, a liturgical book of prayers and blessings, list the signs of possession as "ability to speak with some facility in a strange tongue or to understand it when spoken by another; the faculty of divulging future and hidden events; display of powers which are beyond the subject's age and natural condition" as well as other unspecified evidence.

The rite warns the priest-exorcist to beware of the devil's tricks: Satan may give the appearance of having left a person and may even allow him to receive Communion without any ill effects, the ritual says. But the only sure way for an exorcist to know that he had been successful is to make the demon tell when he is leaving and to give a certain sign.

The Roman Ritual warns against the devil's efforts to get the possessed person to visit a sorcerer or necromancer or perform a superstitious act.

After making the recommended confession and celebrating Mass, the priest, wearing a surplice and purple stole, begins the ceremony by sprinkling holy water and tracing the sign of the cross on himself, the possessed person and a "very limited" number of bystanders. Over 45 signs of the cross are made during the rite.

After the Litany of the Saints and several scripture readings, the priest prays: "I cast you out unclean spirit . . . tremble in fear, Satan, you enemy of faith, you foe of the human race, you begetter of death. . . . Why, then, do you stand and resist, knowing as you must that Christ the Lord brings your plans to nothing?"

The exorcist may continue the prayers, if he sees signs of progress, "for two, three, four hours or longer . . . if he can." Any words which especially torment the evil spirit are repeated often.

Besides holy water, the priest has a crucifix at hand and relics of the saints which must be encased. He may prescribe no medication and may not bring the Holy Eucharist near the possessed person.

During the rite the exorcist may not "digress into senseless prattle" with the demon or try to get the spirit to "answer questions prompted by curiosity." But the exorcist must ask "the number and name" of the spirits, the time they entered and the cause of the possession. Often the rite is repeated for weeks, months or years before the exorcism is successful. (N.C.).

Some Other OSV Paperbacks

ASTROLOGY: FACT OR FICTION? by Kenneth J. Delano. What is the difference between astronomy and astrology? Is astrology legitimate or a great hoax on the public. Read for yourself this fascinating account and then weigh your own conclusions. $1.95 (128 pp)

THE FORTY MARTYRS by Donald Wuerl. "I am a Catholic man and a priest. If you esteem my religion treason, then I am guilty." Thus spoke Edmund Campion just before his execution in London in 1581. Here are the gripping stories of the newly canonized English and Welsh martyrs. $1.25 (80 pp)

THE SEXUAL MARRIAGE. To be a sexual man or woman means to be a total man or woman. The 28 psychologists and marriage counselors who wrote this book give the keys to a more fruitful human relationship. $2.95 (192 pp)

TO SETTLE YOUR CONSCIENCE by Rev. Cass Kucharek. Here are straight answers to hundreds of moral problems that perplex thousands of people, given in attention-holding example style. $3.95 (264 pp)

SEPARATED BRETHREN by William J. Whalen. A survey of Protestant, Anglican, Orthodox, Old Catholic, Jewish, Buddhist, and other denominations and cults in the United States. For those who want to know something about their neighbors' beliefs and practices. $2.95 (304 pp)

JOURNEY INTO THE VOID by Donam Hahn Wakefield. A firsthand study of Buddhism and Christianity based on the author's firsthand study and experience. $1.25 (64 pp)

THE TRIAL OF CHRIST by Ralph Gorman, CP. The author presents strong evidence that it was impossible for the trial and crucifixion of Christ to have taken place in the short period of time traditionally given. A gripping recreation of those events. $2.95 (200 pp)

OUR SUNDAY VISITOR. A weekly news-magazine in tabloid format commenting on current trends and events as they affect religion. Includes youth section; book, television and movie reviews; full color photography. Mailed to your home each week. $8.50 per year.

Order from your booksellers or if not available:

Our Sunday Visitor, Inc.
Huntington, Indiana, 46750